GLOBAL GUARDIANS

HALTING POLLUTION

Keisha Jones

PowerKiDS
press

New York

Published in 2017 by The Rosen Publishing Group, Inc.
29 East 21st Street, New York, NY 10010

First Edition

Editor: Theresa Morlock
Book Design: Reann Nye

Photo Credits: Cover (background), pp. 1–24 (background) jwblinn/ Shutterstock.com; cover (map), pp.1–24 Buslik/Shutterstock.com; cover (top), p. 1 Fotos593/Shutterstock.com; cover (bottom) David Sprott/Shutterstock.com; p. 4 Volt Collection/Shutterstock.com; p. 5 VanderWolf Images/Shutterstock.com; p. 7 (top) Thanatham Piriyakarnjanakul/EyeEm/Getty Images; p. 7 (bottom) J. Lekavicius/Shutterstock.com; p. 9 Richard Packwood/Oxford Scientific/ Getty Images; p. 11 (top) AzleenRamli/Shutterstock.com; p. 11 (bottom) Komsan Loonprom/Shutterstock.com; p. 13 Steve Allen/DigitalVision/ Getty Images; p. 15 (top) SimplyCreativePhotography/E+/Getty Images; p. 15 (bottom) Sean Pavone/Shutterstock.com; p. 17 Microgen/Shutterstock.com; p. 18 Andrey B. Kostin/Shutterstock.com; p. 19 fastfun23/Shutterstock.com; p. 21 (top) Stoyan Yotov/Shutterstock.com; p. 21 (bottom) B.Stefanov/ Shutterstock.com; p. 22 wavebreakmedia/Shutterstock.com.

Cataloging-in-Publication Data

Names: Jones, Keisha.
Title: Halting pollution / Keisha Jones.
Description: New York : PowerKids Press, 2017. | Series: Global guardians| Includes index.
Identifiers: ISBN 9781499427561 (pbk.) | ISBN 9781499429336 (library bound) | ISBN 9781508152743 (6 pack)
Subjects: LCSH: Pollution–Juvenile literature. | Pollution prevention–Juvenile literature.
Classification: LCC TD176.J66 2017 | DDC 363.73–dc23

Manufactured in China

CONTENTS

UNDERSTANDING POLLUTION

Planet Earth is our home, and it's a beautiful one. However, people produce waste that pollutes our world. Cars and factories create gases that make the air dirty. Oil from boats pollutes our waters. Chemicals used by farmers can have harmful effects on the **environment**. Littering also harms Earth.

Pollution hurts plants, animals, and people. It's important to find ways to reduce or halt pollution altogether. Many people recycle their trash. Others help clean polluted rivers and streams. People decide to ride bikes or walk instead of using cars. These may seem like small actions, but they can produce big changes in our environment.

Pollution is anything that makes the air, water, or land unclean.

WHAT'S IN THE AIR?

Pollution is all around us, including in the air we breathe. Both nature and people can pollute the air. Strong winds blow around dirt, while forest fires produce thick smoke. People burn fuel to run cars, heat homes, and produce goods. Burning **fossil fuels** gives off gases that pollute the air. This can hurt our **lungs** and cause sicknesses.

In recent years, people have started to work on the air pollution problem. Car companies are building new cars that produce fewer emissions. Factories are improving their processes to reduce pollution. For example, some power plants use filters to trap pollution before it leaves their chimneys.

CONSERVATION CLUES

Emissions are gases and **particles** put into the air by cars, factories, and other things. Low-emission cars are a more environmentally friendly choice.

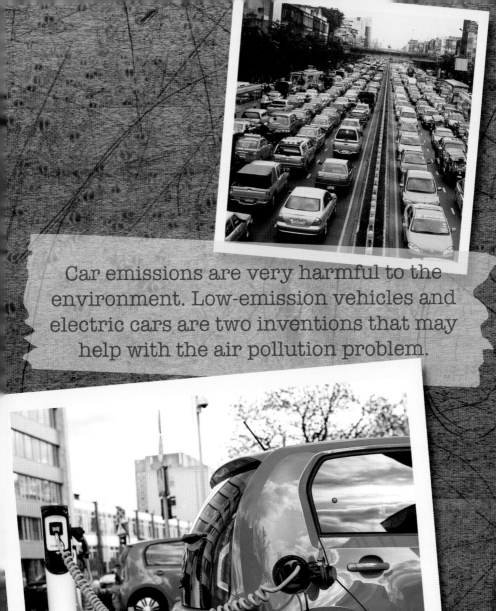

Car emissions are very harmful to the environment. Low-emission vehicles and electric cars are two inventions that may help with the air pollution problem.

RAINING DOWN ACID

Pollution enters the air and joins with other gases and water vapor, which is water in gas form. The mixture becomes acid rain. Acid rain damages the metal on cars, bridges, and railroad tracks. It also eats away at stone.

Acid rain also kills trees and other plants by hurting leaves and washing important **nutrients** out of the soil. Animals are also in danger. Acid rain that falls into lakes can kill fish. Animals that eat the fish, such as eagles and bears, may not have enough food when the fish die. Acid rain is a threat, or danger, to every plant and animal in an ecosystem.

CONSERVATION CLUES

Acid rain can also fall as snow, hail, and fog.

An ecosystem is a community of living creatures and nonliving things and the relationships, or connections, between them. Every creature in an ecosystem depends on the others for survival. When one plant or animal is affected by acid rain, it can harm everything else that's part of the ecosystem.

WHAT'S HAPPENING TO EARTH'S WATERS?

Acid rain is just one of the many things that pollutes water. Factories pollute water when they use it to cool and clean their machines. The machines give off chemicals that are unsafe for animals, plants, and people. In our homes, we pollute water when we shower or use the toilet.

All living things need clean water to drink. When we drink polluted water, we can become very sick. Animals can get sick and die, too. Many groups, including the Environmental Protection Agency (EPA), are working to clean Earth's waters. They know that if we don't have clean water, all living creatures will be in trouble.

CONSERVATION CLUES

A 2010 oil spill in the Gulf of Mexico was the worst oil spill in U.S. history. An estimated 3.19 million barrels worth of oil leaked into the gulf, harming fish, birds, shrimp, dolphins, and more.

Before 1972, farmers used a **pesticide** called DDT to kill bugs that ate their plants. The DDT washed into lakes and killed fish and the animals that ate them. This caused such harm to the environment that using DDT became illegal in 1972.

HAZARDS TO HUMANS

The term "hazardous waste" sounds scary, and rightfully so. People use some things that are considered hazardous waste, such as cell phones and bug sprays. They should not be thrown away in the regular trash. Hazardous waste requires special care to avoid polluting the environment.

Radioactive waste is another kind of hazardous material. It comes from power plants that make nuclear energy. Nuclear energy is energy that comes from breaking **atoms** apart. Power plants get rid of their waste in strong containers lined with steel. People should never come into contact with radioactive waste. It makes people very, very sick.

CONSERVATION CLUES

Radioactive material or radiation can cause terrible sicknesses, such as cancer.

Containers for nuclear waste are called
spent fuel pools. They're made of a
stone mixture called concrete that's
several feet thick and lined with steel.

BETTERING THE BROWNFIELDS

Some pollution comes from businesses in our towns and cities. Factories, paper mills, gas stations, and even dry cleaners are businesses that may pollute the land around them. This kind of polluted land is called a brownfield. When businesses leave, the land can't be used again until it's cleaned up.

Many communities are making an effort to clean up brownfields. It's costly, but it's worth it. The city of Atlanta, Georgia, turned the land that once belonged to Atlantic Steel into an area for houses, offices, stores, and parks. Brownfields in Seattle, Washington, and Pittsburgh, Pennsylvania, have also been **repurposed** for people to enjoy.

CONSERVATION CLUES

Typical chemicals found in a brownfield include lead, pesticides, asbestos, and other harmful matter.

Over the years, the EPA has launched programs to encourage cities and towns to clean up brownfields and turn them into land a community can use. This creates jobs and helps the economy, too.

Atlantic Station in Atlanta, Georgia, is a redeveloped brownfield.

SCIENTISTS TO THE RESCUE!

Some scientists and researchers spend their career studying pollution. Environmental scientists and biologists measure and track different kinds of pollution, searching for answers to our problems. Scientists check for acid by measuring a body of water's pH level. Low pH levels mean there's more acid in the water. Fish, frogs, and other animals can die if the water they live in is too acidic.

Special tools help scientists measure pollution in the sky. Planes with special labs allow scientists to test for chemicals in the air. However, regular people can track air pollution, too! There are many **sensors** you can buy to help.

CONSERVATION CLUES

An air quality monitor can track how much pollution you're exposed to, or around, in any given day.

The hard work of scientists and environmental activists has helped us learn about the dangers of pollution.

FIXING THE PROBLEM

Governments fight pollution by making laws to prevent it. In 1963, the United States Congress passed the Clean Air Act. This law limits the amount of pollution that cars, factories, and power plants can put in the air. In 1972, Congress passed the Clean Water Act, which tells companies they can only put a certain amount of waste into U.S. waters.

While some pollution laws are written for big businesses, other laws are made for people. In many states, it's against the law to smoke in restaurants and other public buildings. This keeps the air cleaner.

Cigarette smoke is very bad for your health, even if you're not a smoker. Anti-smoking laws help keep everyone safe.

HELPING EARTH

Scientists and governments are working hard to halt pollution. You can help by making your community friendlier to the environment and the creatures that live in it.

Keep your water clean by learning how to safely get rid of cleaners and other materials such as paint and oil. Get your friends together and spend a day picking up trash in a local park. Talk to your family about riding bikes and walking instead of taking your car. When everyone pitches in, our planet will be a safer place for all living things.

CONSERVATION CLUES

A lot of our trash goes to landfills. Landfills can release harmful chemicals into our soil and water. Modern landfills are built to hold garbage and protect the environment at the same time.

Recycling paper, cans, and bottles is a great way to help the environment. Recycling reduces, or lowers, the amount of waste we send to landfills.

DOING YOUR PART

It's everyone's job to help the environment. Governments and communities fight pollution in different ways. The United States' Superfund program helps people clean up hazardous waste. A group of people from South Carolina worked with Superfund to clean up chemical and radioactive wastes a factory had dumped near the Savannah River. Together, they addressed the land and water pollution around the river.

We're still learning a lot about pollution, but one thing is certain: pollution will not go away on its own. Everyone must take action to stop it. While you may not think you can do a lot on your own, together, people can do great things!

GLOSSARY

atom: The smallest unit of matter.

environment: The natural surroundings of a person, plant, or animal.

fossil fuel: A fuel, such as coal, oil, or natural gas, that is formed in the earth from dead plants or animals.

lungs: The parts of the body we use to breathe.

nutrients: Tiny particles in the soil that plants need to be healthy.

particle: A tiny part of matter.

pesticide: A chemical used to harm bugs or other creatures that harm plants and animals.

radioactive: Having to do with the dangerous rays and particles given off by certain unstable kinds of atoms.

repurpose: To find another use for something.

sensor: A tool that tests for or measures something and records or responds to it.

23

INDEX

WEBSITES

Due to the changing nature of Internet links, PowerKids Press has developed an online list of websites related to the subject of this book. This site is updated regularly. Please use this link to access the list: www.powerkidslinks.com/glob/poll